THE OFFICIAL GUIDE TO THE
JURASSIC COAST

DORSET AND EAST DEVON'S WORLD HERITAGE COAST

A WALK THROUGH TIME

Edited by Professor Denys Brunsden

A Coastal Publishing Limited Book

Project Editor Professor Denys Brunsden
Edited and written by Tim Badman, Denys Brunsden,
Richard Edmonds, Sally King, Chris Pamplin, Malcolm Turnbull
Design Jonathan Lewis
Production Peter Sills

First Published in 2003
Reprinted with minor amendments 2005, 2008, 2013 and 2015
Coastal Publishing Limited
The Studio, Puddletown Road, Wareham, Dorset BH20 6AE
Tel: 01929 554195
email: enquiries@coastalpublishing.co.uk
www.coastalpublishing.co.uk

ISBN 978-0-9544845-0-7

British Library Cataloguing-in-Publication Data
A catalogue record for this book is available from the British Library.

Any views or opinions expressed in this publication are solely those of the
authors and do not necessarily represent those of the publisher.

In the interests of your personal safety and enjoyment of the World Heritage Coast, the
Jurassic Coast Trust and Coastal Publishing Limited recommend that you follow fully all the
relevant safety advice in this book and the Fossil and The Countryside Codes. The Jurassic
Coast Trust and Coastal Publishing Limited can accept no liability whatsoever.

Your purchase of this book helps to support the conservation and education
programmes of the Jurassic Coast Trust (Registered Charity No: 1101134).
www.jurassiccoast.org/get-involved

BP is proud of its association with the World Heritage coastline and is pleased
to be supportive in the development of the first edition of this publication.

Front cover image: Mupe Rocks near Lulworth Cove

Printed and bound in the United Kingdom.

Coastal Publishing Limited and the authors have made every reasonable effort to
locate, contact and acknowledge copyright owners and wishes to be informed by any
copyright owners who are not properly identified and acknowledged so that we can
make any necessary corrections.

Acknowledgements

We are grateful to BP for generous sponsorship of the first edition of this
guide, and to Dorset County Council, Devon County Council, Natural
England for financial support.

Much of this guide is distilled from the World Heritage Site nomination
published in 2000, to which over 60 scientists contributed information
and advice. We are grateful to all those whose input has been used
in this guide and to all those who supplied images. We would like to
thank the members of the World Heritage Steering Group, Science and
Conservation Advisory Group and Tourism Working Group for their
advice, and the following people who reviewed part or all of the
completed book, or assisted with its production: David Andrew, Penny
Bayer, Adrian Brokenshire, Dick Burt, Nic Butler, Paul Ensom, Jane
Francis, Ramues Gallois, Lesley Garlick, Malcolm Hart, John Hayes, Trev
Haysom, Alan Holiday, David Jenkins, Albert Knott, Jonathan Larwood,
John Lowe, Kirstie McConnell, Major Mansel, Paul Matthews, Major
Nelson, Vincent May, Don Moxom, Maddy Pfaff, Robin Plowman,
Michael Poultney, David Richards, Richard Scrivener, David Sole, Mandy
Staple, Cheryl Stapleton, Peter Tinsley, Hugh Torrens, Jan Turnbull, John
Varley, Geoff Warrington, James Weld, John Whittaker, Simon Williams,
Patrick Woodford.

Image Acknowledgements
(Key: t:top; m:middle; b:bottom; l:left; r:right; c:centre)

Images in this book are copyright of the photographers and artists.

Photos: All aerial photography of the World Heritage Site was taken by Peter
Sills: coastalpublishing.co.uk. Other photography by Peter Sills, except: Mike
Askew:14mr; Tim Badman:23ml; 33br; 45tl; 53tr; Beer Quarry Caves:33t; Bristol
Museum:17tr; 37m; Denys Brunsden: 23b; Charmouth Heritage Coast Centre:
21tr, mr, br; Chesil and the Fleet Reserve: 43tl, tr; Devon County Council: 26bl;
Dorset County Council:58tr; Richard Edmonds: 13mr; 17tl; 19c; 23tr, mr, mc;
27mr, br; 30-31; 31tr, br; 38; 39ml; 41tr, mr; 42t; 44b; 45tc, tr, br; 47t, b; 50m,
55bl, 57mr, 62b; English Nature:43tc; Paul Ensom:19br; Jean Flower:27l; Jane
Francis:50bl; Malcolm Hart: 15tr; Jonathan Lewis:, Cover; 4-5; 21bl: 28-29; 42-43:
46-47: 52-53; 54; 60-61; Jurassic Coast Team:, 62tr, mr, br; Natural History
Museum:36mr; Chris Pamplin:27tr, mr; 28bl; 33bl; Sam Rose: 6tr; Dennis Smaile
Collection:54t; 55mr; David Sole: 37br; Terry Sweeney:9l; Malcolm Turnbull:
56ml; UNESCO:7ml-mr; West Dorset District Council:9r; June Woodger: 21ml.

Illustrations by Jonathan Lewis, except: David Scammell: 12m; Paleomap Project:
14t, 16t, 18t; Dineley and Metcalf: 15t; Courtesy of Bristol University, painted by
Pam Baldaro: 15b; John Sibbick: 17; Dorset County Council: 19; Bill Bennett: 40l,
49mr; Geological Society Collection: 36t; Lyme Regis Museum: 36br; National
Museum of Wales collection 37t; Anthea Dunkley 50t.

The poem on page 10 was written for the Site by local poet Peneli.

CONTENTS

The Dorset and East Devon Coast has been known for years as a place of great beauty, but it also has a value that is of truly global importance.

In December 2001 the 'Jurassic Coast' was awarded World Heritage Site status and became recognised as a place of outstanding universal value. Its 155 kilometres of dramatic cliffs, tumbling landslides, spectacular arches and sea stacks display 185 million years of the Earth's history, and countless beautifully preserved fossils enable us to reconstruct the evolution of life. It is a place of understanding and enjoyment, a scientific asset and an educational resource.

We should all feel proud of the coast's new status and I applaud Dorset and Devon County Councils and the Dorset Coast Forum for having the vision to seek it and the application to achieve it. They recognise that protection of the environment is both fundamental to the quality of all our lives and vital for the local, rural economy.

When I officially opened the Site in October 2002, I had the opportunity to see for myself the truly outstanding beauty of this dramatic coastline. I hope that World Heritage status will inspire many more people to visit the 'Jurassic Coast' and, in doing so, to learn about the history of our Earth. This guide is an important step in that direction.

On Thursday 3rd October 2002 His Royal Highness The Prince of Wales unveiled two specially commissioned stone markers at Orcombe Point and Lulworth Cove to mark the inauguration of the World Heritage Site.

" *What will be the future of this ... coastline,
so richly endowed as a training ground and
museum of geology? Few tracts of equal
size could raise so many claims, scientific,
aesthetic and literary, for preservation ... If
the English of the present generation allow
this heritage of the community to be
irreparably spoilt for private gain they
will be held by posterity to have been
unworthy to possess it.*"

W.J. Arkell, From *Geology of the country around Weymouth,
Swanage, Corfe and Lulworth* 1947.
Arkell was author of Jurassic Geology of the World, published in 1956.

This guide is dedicated to the memory of
Michael House and with thanks to all those
who have worked and are working to make
Arkell's vision a reality.

Welcome to the Dorset and East Devon Coast

This is England's first natural World Heritage Site, and is known as the 'Jurassic Coast'. The Site includes 95 miles (155 km) of unspoilt cliffs and beaches from Exmouth in East Devon, through West Dorset, Weymouth and Portland, to end near Old Harry Rocks in Purbeck.

The Dorset and East Devon Coast is beautiful, but the main reason for its inscription on the World Heritage List is its unique insight into the Earth Sciences. The rocks record 185 million years of the Earth's history. The Site's unique value creates a 'walk through time' that includes the Triassic, Jurassic and Cretaceous Periods. The varied geology also provides a spectacular laboratory of coastal change, and supports rare and important plants and animals. It is a place to be enjoyed, learnt from and looked after for future generations.

The skull of the Weymouth Bay Pliosaur discovered between 2005 and 2008 is one of the largest and certainly one of the best preserved examples ever found in the world. At 2.4 m long, the whole animal would have been 15 to 18 m in length and with such massive jaws it was the scariest sea creature to have ever lived in all time.

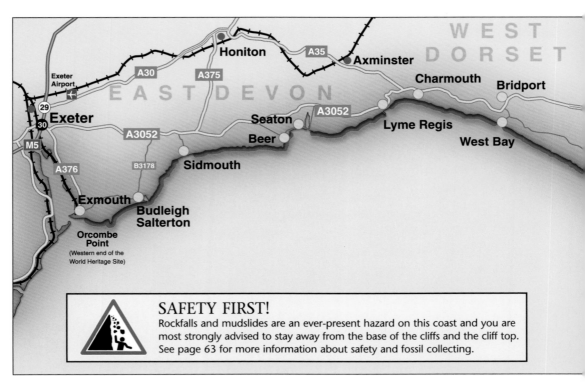

SAFETY FIRST!

Rockfalls and mudslides are an ever-present hazard on this coast and you are most strongly advised to stay away from the base of the cliffs and the cliff top. See page 63 for more information about safety and fossil collecting.

What is a World Heritage Site?

World Heritage Sites are places of 'outstanding universal value', recognised as part of the heritage of all mankind. They are carefully selected by UNESCO (United Nations Educational, Scientific and Cultural Organisation). When the Dorset and East Devon Coast was designated a World Heritage Site in December 2001, it joined a select group of globally important natural and cultural Sites, which includes the Great Barrier Reef, the Grand Canyon, the Taj Mahal and the Great Wall of China. World Heritage status means that Sites should be protected, conserved, presented and passed intact to future generations.

United Nations
Educational, Scientific and
Cultural Organization

Dorset and East Devon Coast
inscribed on the World
Heritage List in 2001

UNESCO's World Heritage Emblem is used to recognise World Heritage Sites throughout the world. Designed by Michel Olyff, the Emblem symbolizes the interdependence of cultural and natural properties: the central square is a form created by man and the circle represents nature, the two being intimately linked. The Emblem is round, like the world, but at the same time it is a symbol of protection.

The Grand Canyon.

The Great Barrier Reef.

The Great Wall of China.

The Taj Mahal.

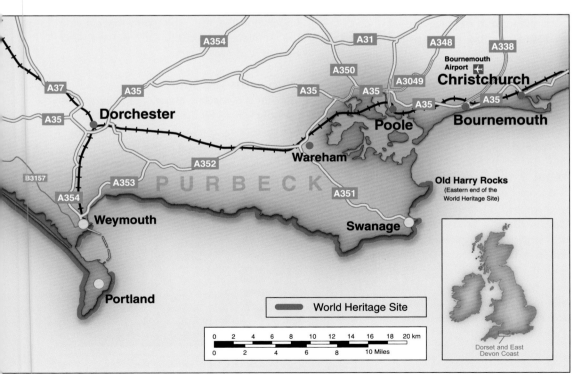

Please refer to the back of this guide for a larger scale fold-out map.

THE WORLD HERITAGE SITE

Understanding the Site

World Heritage Status is all about protecting and conserving an exceptional place and presenting it to visitors. Each part of the Dorset and East Devon Coast has distinctive interests and issues. The Site sits within protected country-side and adjacent to towns and villages, which also form an essential part of its story. This page provides a simple introduction to the Site, and how it is managed.

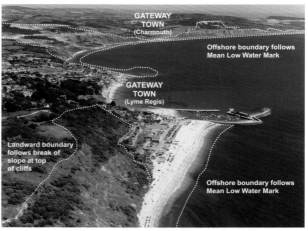

The Site boundary around Lyme Regis, showing the narrow extent of the World Heritage Site and the link to the Gateway Towns.

What is the Dorset and East Devon Coast World Heritage Site?

The World Heritage Site is a coastal strip of land, around 95 miles (155 km) in length. It is a narrow Site, lying between the top of the cliffs and the low water mark. It was declared a World Heritage Site by UNESCO on 13th December 2001, as:

' An outstanding example representing major stages of the Earth's history, including the record of life, significant ongoing geological processes in the development of landforms, and significant geomorphic or physiographic features.'

What is the Jurassic Coast?

The Dorset and East Devon Coast World Heritage Site is popularly known as the 'Jurassic Coast'. The name comes from the best known of the geological periods found within it, but in fact the Site includes rocks from the Triassic, Jurassic and Cretaceous Periods. Together these periods make up the Mesozoic Era of geological time, between 250 and 65 million years ago.

What is the 'World Heritage Coast'?

This is an informal term used to include both the World Heritage Site, and the immediate towns and countryside which provide the education, accommodation and transport facilities that enable people to visit and understand the Site. The towns that provide the immediate services to the Site have been termed 'Gateway Towns'.

Who owns the Site?

The Site is owned by many landowners. The majority is held by the National Trust, large private estates, the Ministry of Defence, the Crown Estate and local authorities.

About one third of the World Heritage Site is owned by the National Trust, including large estates in West Dorset and Purbeck.

How is the World Heritage Site conserved?

All of the land in the World Heritage Site has legal protection under UK Acts of Parliament. The site includes 13 geological and biological Sites of Special Scientific Interest (SSSIs), which are regulated by English Nature, the government conservation agency. The SSSIs encompass 66 identified localities of national and international importance for the earth sciences. Most of the Site also lies within the East Devon Area of Outstanding Natural Beauty (AONB) and the Dorset AONB. These two designated areas recognise nationally important landscapes, conserving both the Site and the wider countryside that surrounds it.

Monitoring coastal change in West Dorset using satellite technology.

The footpath network leading to the Site needs regular maintenance.

How is the Site managed?

A Management Plan has been agreed for the World Heritage Site. This is the key document which establishes the policies for the Site, and the arrangements for co-ordinating effort between all the different interests who have responsibilities for it. The plan sets out proposals for conservation, access, education and science. It also identifies ways in which World Heritage status can help sustainable development in the wider area of Dorset and East Devon.

The future of the World Heritage Site is an exciting long-term commitment for the whole area, involving thousands of people helping to conserve and celebrate the coast. The aim is to pass the Site on to future generations to experience, learn from and enjoy in the same way that we are able to do today.

For more information please visit
www.jurassiccoast.org

Animations of coastal processes
Details on Site conservation
Groups to join to find out more about geology
Educational case studies about the coast
Useful publications
Links to other World Heritage Sites
And much more!

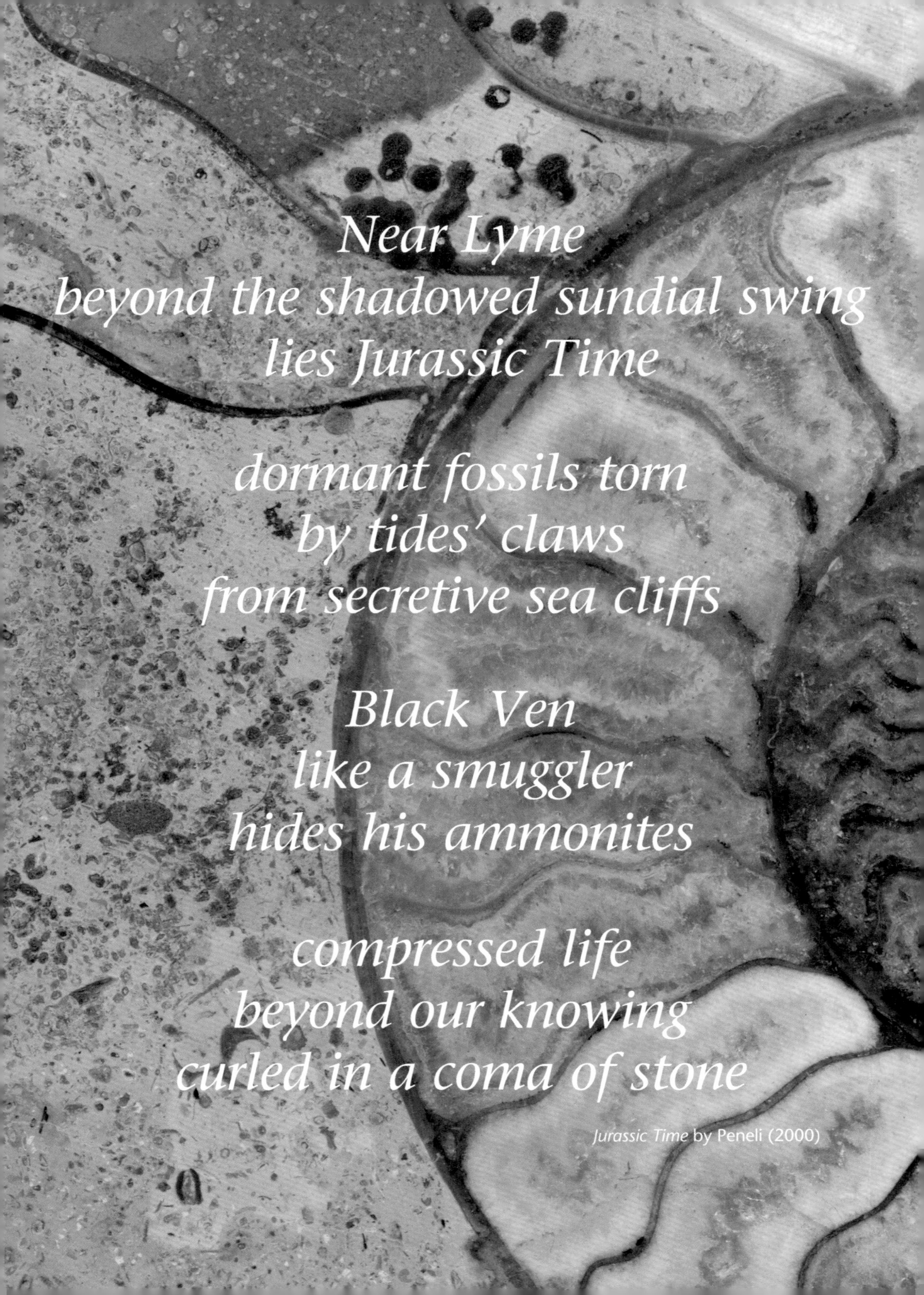

Near Lyme
beyond the shadowed sundial swing
lies Jurassic Time

dormant fossils torn
by tides' claws
from secretive sea cliffs

Black Ven
like a smuggler
hides his ammonites

compressed life
beyond our knowing
curled in a coma of stone

Jurassic Time by Peneli (2000)

STORIES OF TIME

The theme that runs through the World Heritage Site is the discovery of 'deep time'. The Site is a spectacular record of changes that took place over millions of years, the creation of rocks, landforms and the evolution of species. It is also a story of the birth of a science.

Our World Heritage Story

The story of the Dorset and East Devon Coast begins 250 million years ago. The rocks record the Mesozoic Era - the 'Middle Ages' of life on Earth - comprising the Triassic, Jurassic and Cretaceous Periods of geological time. Today the spectacular geology is beautifully exposed and accessible within the World Heritage Site.

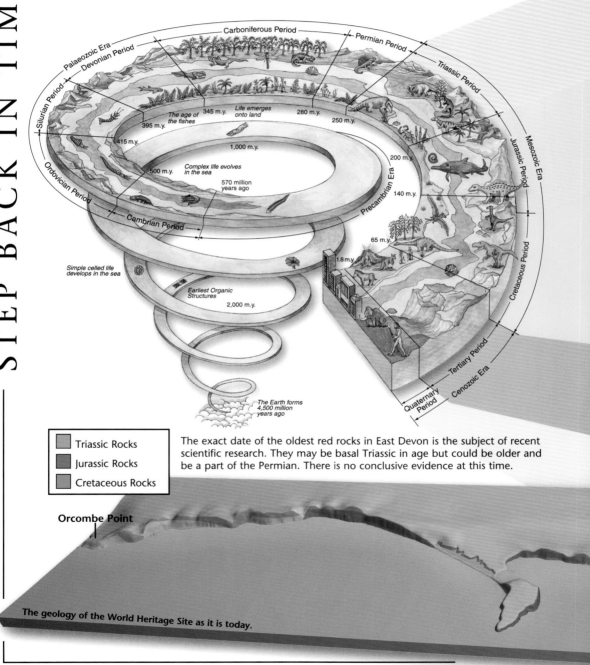

- Triassic Rocks
- Jurassic Rocks
- Cretaceous Rocks

The exact date of the oldest red rocks in East Devon is the subject of recent scientific research. They may be basal Triassic in age but could be older and be a part of the Permian. There is no conclusive evidence at this time.

Orcombe Point

The geology of the World Heritage Site as it is today.

West   East

Triassic Period (250-200 million years ago):
Rocks form in desert conditions. Vast rivers
flow through baking deserts depositing thick
layers of pebbles and sand. Huge shallow lakes
spill across the desert plains.

Jurassic Period (200-140 million years ago):
Sea levels rise, flooding the deserts. Ammonites,
marine reptiles and other life flourish in the
tropical seas. A thick sequence of clays,
sandstones and limestones is deposited.

Cretaceous Period (140-65 million years ago): Sea levels drop in the early
Cretaceous. Rocks form in swamps, forests and lagoons (a). Earth movements
then tilt all the rocks to the east (b), and the rock layers are eroded (c).

Sea levels rise again later in
the Cretaceous, depositing clays, sandstones
and the Chalk in deepening marine conditions.

Tertiary Period (65-1.8 million years ago):
After the Mesozoic Era, mammals come
to dominate life on Earth. Massive earth
movements form the Alps, and create a
great fold through Purbeck. The plateaus
of East Devon and Dorset are uplifted.

Old Harry
Rocks

Quaternary Period (1.8 million years ago to the present): Erosion creates
the hills and valleys of the present landscape. A series of ice ages and rapid
changes in sea level take place. In the last glacial period sea level drops
to 140 metres lower than today. The last ice age ends 10,000 years
ago, and sea levels rise to create the modern coastline.

STEP BACK IN TIME

The Triassic World (250-200 million years ago)

In Triassic times, the World Heritage Site was part of a super-continent called Pangaea. This landmass divided to form the continents of the modern world. Dorset and East Devon lay within the arid centre of the super-continent and hot, desert conditions prevailed. A huge mountain chain lay to the west. The mountains were gradually eroded and their roots remain in Dartmoor and Brittany. Rivers flowed north and east, depositing pebbles and sand across southern England. The rivers spilled into the desert, creating vast lakes that were subject to evaporation.

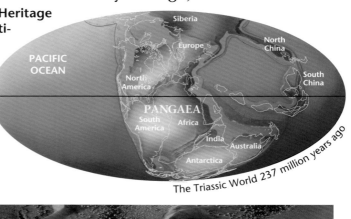

The Triassic World 237 million years ago

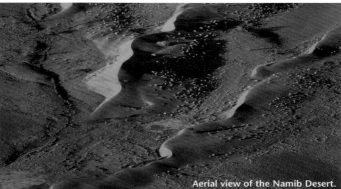

Aerial view of the Namib Desert.

The Triassic rocks in the World Heritage Site are red because deserts contain very little organic material and, in its absence, iron forms red oxides. In our modern world the Namib Desert in Africa has the sort of conditions that once existed in East Devon.

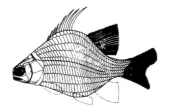

Triassic Life

The Triassic is a critical period of evolution. Life on Earth had been decimated by a large mass extinction event at the end of the previous period. Surviving groups of animals evolved and diversified. The first dinosaurs evolved and went on to dominate life during the Mesozoic Era. Most of our living groups of four-legged animals had arrived by the end of the Triassic, including frogs, turtles and crocodiles. The first true mammals also evolved during the Triassic.

Fossils in the Triassic rocks are rare and generally poorly preserved. Occasionally important finds are made, such as this fine skeleton of the mid-Triassic reptile, *Rhynchosaurus*. Ten species of reptiles, amphibians and fish have been found on the East Devon coast within the World Heritage Site, making it the richest mid-Triassic fossil site in Britain.

A reconstruction of Mid-Triassic times in East Devon, based on fossils found in East Devon. A scorpion in the foreground contemplates a pair of small reptiles on the rocks. To the right is a hefty amphibian. Two rhynchosaurs stand in the background, and behind them are two of another kind of reptile, called rauisuchians.

The Jurassic World (200-140 million years ago)

Pangaea started to break apart during the Jurassic Period. The Atlantic Ocean opened to the west of Britain and the Americas drifted away from Europe. The Earth was relatively warm, sea levels were high and there were hardly any polar ice caps. The Jurassic rocks of Dorset and East Devon record marine conditions during the Jurassic Period - conditions that fluctuated from relatively deep seas to coastal swamps. Sea levels rose and fell in a series of cycles, depositing deep water clays, followed by sandstones and finally shallow water limestones. Seas were shallower in the Middle Jurassic, creating an environment of islands surrounded by shallow shoals, similar to the Caribbean of today. Seas then deepened again, and finally shallowed towards the end of the Jurassic, creating the conditions for a forest to flourish in a tropical swamp environment.

The Jurassic World 152 million years ago

The clays at the base of Golden Cap formed in the Jurassic seas around 185 million years ago.

Jurassic Life

Ammonites were molluscs related to the modern squid, but usually had hard spiral shells. Many species of ammonite fossils are found on the Dorset and East Devon Coast. The giant ammonite, *Titanites* (below) comes from Portland.

A reconstruction of *Dimorphodon*, a Jurassic flying reptile about the size of a crow. This species was first found at Lyme Regis by the great fossil hunter Mary Anning in 1828.

The expansion of shallow seas encouraged an explosion of life in the Jurassic, and many animals evolved rapidly in order to take advantage of the new habitats available. Reptiles were the 'top predators' on land, sea and in the air. Dinosaurs walked the Earth and the dominant carnivores in the seas included ichthyosaurs, plesiosaurs and crocodiles. This reconstruction shows ichthyosaurs and a shoal of fish swimming in the shallow seas of the Jurassic Coast, around 195 million years ago, and is drawn from local fossil finds.

THE JURASSIC PERIOD

The Cretaceous World (140-65 million years ago)

During the Cretaceous Period, America continued to drift away from Europe, and the Atlantic started to become a recognisable ocean. Early in the Cretaceous, the environment of the World Heritage Site was similar to the modern Gulf of Arabia, with lagoons covered by salt flats known as sabkhas. Conditions became more hospitable, with lush swamps populated by dinosaurs. Mid-way through the period, earth movements deep under south-west England tilted the rocks to the east. Then, as the Atlantic Ocean and Mediterranean expanded, a vast sea developed over the area. Within the clear, warm waters billions of microscopic algae bloomed, and their skeletons sank to the sea floor to form the pure, white Chalk.

The Cretaceous World 94 million years ago

The Great Unconformity

The 'Great Unconformity', a time gap between rocks of different age, runs right across the World Heritage Site. The rocks were tilted east in the Mid-Cretaceous, and then eroded by seas and rivers. There was little erosion in the east of the Site but in the west, all the Jurassic and Lower Cretaceous rocks are missing and the Upper Cretaceous rocks lie directly on the eroded surface of the Triassic. So the walk through time is a little more complex: because both the oldest and some of the youngest rocks in the Site are found in East Devon.

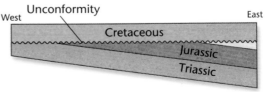

Both the colour and the shape of the cliffs show the position of the unconformity at Branscombe (above) and Golden Cap (left).

Cretaceous Life

The Cretaceous is the time when some of the largest and most fearsome dinosaurs walked the Earth and is also the period when the first flowering plants evolved. The end of the Cretaceous is critical to the shape of the modern world (though not recorded in the World Heritage Site). A mass extinction took place which brought to an end the reign of the reptiles as the dominant life on Earth. The dinosaurs, great marine reptiles and the ammonites were amongst the species which became extinct. The world that would follow saw the present style of life on Earth emerge, dominated by mammals, flowering plants and grasses.

Purbeck rocks near Durlston.

This reconstruction dramatises the Purbeck environment 135 million years ago, with large *Iguanodon* and smaller dinosaurs living in the coastal swamps.

The earliest Cretaceous rocks in the World Heritage Site are the Purbeck Beds, perhaps the most complex rock sequence within the entire coast. They contain a wealth of fossils including dinosaur footprints and the microscopic teeth of early mammals.

The Chalk at White Nothe.

Chalk

The Chalk is the youngest Cretaceous rock in the World Heritage Site and is found throughout the area. Animals such as this sea urchin burrowed in the sediment of the Chalk sea floor.

THE CRETACEOUS PERIOD

A diversity of landforms

Coastal processes have acted on the rocks to create an enormous variety of coastal landforms - cliffs, beaches, landslides, stacks, arches, bays and caves of unparalleled diversity.

The Purbeck coast is a classic place to see how the resistance of different rock types controls the coastal form.

Understanding coastal change

The varied geology of the coast has produced a spectacular laboratory for the modern science of geomorphology - the study of the shape of the land, and the processes that create it. Coastal landforms are changing all the time under the attack of the sea, frost, rain and human activity. The modern study of geomorphology looks at how events of different frequencies and sizes produce change. Small changes, occurring frequently over long periods of time can be just as significant as major events, such as landslides or storms, in creating the shape of the coast. All that is needed is time!

Stacks like these at Ladram Bay are formed where the sea erodes coastal rocks over thousands of years and isolates pieces of cliff.

Chesil Beach is the largest barrier beach and lagoon system in Western Europe. It is believed to have formed over the last 10,000 years.

Coastal change can be rapid and dangerous. This dramatic cliff fall at Stonebarrow in West Dorset, was captured on film in 2000.

A crucible of knowledge

In the early nineteenth century geology was the 'queen of sciences', with a profile in public life equivalent to genetics or the study of space in our modern age. The evidence of the fossil record and the shape of landforms created searching debate. Scientists sought to reconcile the geological evidence with the biblical history of the world - then reckoned to be little more than 6,000 years old with a landscape shaped by Noah's flood. Dorset and East Devon was a crucible for this debate, and some of the major figures who studied the evidence coming from the coast are shown below.

Dr William Smith (1769 - 1839)
Author of the first geological map of England. He drained land in Purbeck circa 1800 and worked in Weymouth in 1812.

Professor William Buckland (1784 - 1856)
Professor of Geology at Oxford. A series of visits to the Site. Used valleys in East Devon and Dorset as examples of the action of Noah's flood.

Professor Adam Sedgwick (1785 - 1873)
Professor of Geology at Cambridge. Visited and bought fossils from Mary Anning.

Rev William Conybeare (1787 - 1857)
Author of the first scientific description of a landslide, at Bindon in East Devon. Vicar at Axmouth between 1836-44.

Dr Gideon Mantell (1790 - 1852)
Discoverer of *Iguanodon*. Visited in 1832 and wrote accounts of excursions on the Dorset Coast.

Sir Roderick Impey Murchison (1792 - 1871)
President of the Geological and Royal Geographical Societies. Visited the coast, and invited Mary Anning to London for her only visit there in 1829.

Sir Henry de la Beche (1796 - 1855)
Founder of the British Geological Survey. Moved to Lyme Regis in 1812, writing a series of papers and publishing *Duria Antiquior*, the first diorama of a past world.

Sir Charles Lyell (1797 - 1875)
Pioneer of the theory that modern processes operated in the geological past.

Mary Anning (1799 - 1847)
A poor woman from Dorset who became known as the 'greatest fossilist that ever lived'. Finder of the first marine reptile skeletons to come to scientific attention.

Professor Richard Owen (1804 - 1892)
Superintendent of the Natural History Museum in London. Seminal paper on the early mammals of Purbeck. Defined the name dinosaur in 1842.

Professor Louis Agassiz (1807 - 1873)
Swiss pioneer of the study of glaciation. Visited in 1834, and named two fossil fish after Mary Anning - the only fossils named after her during her lifetime.

Samuel Husbands Beckles (1814 - 1890)
Excavated fossil mammals at Swanage, under the advice of Owen.

1760 1770 1780 1790 1800 1810 1820 1830 1840 1850 1860 1870 1880 1890 1900

1859 Charles Darwin's 'On the Origin of Species' published

22

The outdoor classroom

From the early days of geology to the present day, the Dorset and East Devon Coast has been a place of discovery. Scientists, researchers, students and conservationists have visited, learnt and gone away enriched. Today the Jurassic Coast is visited by millions of people including tens of thousands of students every year. Many of the coastal centres provide organised visits for schools and walks for the public.

The Lulworth Education Ranger leads one of the many school groups that visit the Site every year.

Discovering fossils.

Fossil ripple marks on Portland.

Geologists at work in Purbeck.

The fascination of looking for fossils on the shoreline continues undiminished since 1858.

THE WALK
THROUGH TIME

*Each gateway to the coast introduces
a new story, exciting discoveries and a
different perspective on time. This
section highlights, from west to east,
the unfolding interests in the
'Walk through Time'.*

Tread softly...
Breathe deeply...

The Triassic Coast

Dramatic cliffs of red rock are the distinctive feature of the East Devon Coast. This is the 'Triassic Coast', and the geology here records conditions on land between 250 and 200 million years ago. Although most of the Triassic rocks do not contain fossils, they do display many clues that enable us to reconstruct a series of desert environments, with sand dunes, salt lakes, lagoons and rivers.

The rusty reds and oranges of the Triassic rocks are due to their origin. Iron minerals have weathered to produce the spectacular colour of the cliffs, and this is the tell-tale sign for geologists that these rocks formed on land in hot, arid conditions. At Exmouth, Budleigh Salterton and Sidmouth there are clues to the different environments that existed when East Devon was a desert.

The 'Geoneedle' at Orcombe Point, was unveiled by HRH Prince of Wales in 2002 to inaugurate the World Heritage Site.

The Triassic Coast looking towards High Peak and Sidmouth. Triassic rocks are beautifully exposed and visible from the coast path along this rugged coastline. Access to the shore on this stretch is possible at Ladram Bay and Sidmouth. Elsewhere the sheer cliffs and beaches are inaccessible, but can be viewed from boat trips that run from Exmouth.

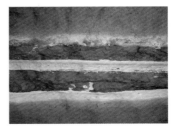

Light coloured bands in the strata at Exmouth indicate slow deposition and the presence of plant life.

The rocks at Exmouth, Budleigh Salterton and Sidmouth show features from deserts. The cross bedding in this picture tells us that large rivers flowed here at this time.

Although fossils in the Triassic red rocks are rare, they are very important. Remains of reptiles, amphibians and fish have been found. Please report any finds to the World Heritage Team.

Veins of the mineral gypsum can be seen on the beach at Weston Mouth, east of Sidmouth. It formed in lakes in the desert, where minerals crystallised as the Sun evaporated the water in temporary desert lakes and salt flats.

Ancient pebbles

Budleigh Salterton has one of the oldest stories within the World Heritage Site - a story that is also spread out along the length of this coast and beyond!

To the west of the sea front lie the famous Budleigh Salterton Pebble Beds. The pebbles are composed of hard quartzite identical to 440 million year old rocks found in Northern France. The pebbles were formed and transported in one of the giant rivers that flowed into the Triassic desert about 240 million years ago.

Over the last few thousand years the pebbles have been falling from the cliffs and today form the bulk of the beach at Budleigh Salterton. The larger cobbles and pebbles are very hard and unlike any other rock type found in Southern England. As a result they survive as they are transported along the coast by the waves. They can be found from Slapton Sands in Devon to Hastings in Sussex.

Pebbles from the ancient rivers were sealed in the rocks which form the cliffs at Budleigh Salterton. Erosion is now releasing them onto the beach so for safety the cliffs should be viewed from a distance.

Pebbles on the beach

Beaches are found throughout the World Heritage Site. At Budleigh the beach is made almost entirely of pebbles eroded from the local cliffs. Other beaches on the coast are made from different materials, mainly flint and chert.

Budleigh Salterton pebbles are often a perfect oval shape and vary in colour from red to pink, ochre to grey. The surfaces are smooth but there are often patterns of bedding while some have veins of white or buff coloured quartz running across them.

Flints originate in the Chalk and are typically white on the surface with a black or brown 'core'. Flint is a hard rock made of silica that originated from sponges and plankton.

Cherts, like flint, are made of silica. They vary in colour and texture and the original sand grains can remain visible. Chert tends to be more massive and blocky than flint.

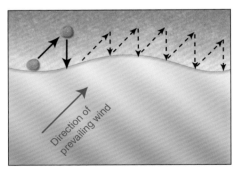

Longshore Drift

Pebbles move along the beach when waves strike the beach at an angle. The pebbles are carried up the beach in the same direction as the wave before being dragged down the beach as the water drains away. So the pebbles move in a saw shaped pattern along the beach.

Direction of prevailing wind

The Unconformity

The coast around Sidmouth offers beautiful coastal scenery and rich geology. The red rocks, capped by yellow Upper Greensand and white Chalk, dominate the views.

In this part of the World Heritage Site the Jurassic rocks have been completely eroded away and a well marked and dramatic 'unconformity' occurs between the Triassic and much younger Cretaceous rocks.

The surrounding hills form a plateau rising inland from 200 to 350 metres. This is an ancient land surface produced by erosion over 40 million years ago in a tropical climate.

Cretaceous Upper Greensand forms the cliff tops east of Sidmouth. Locally it is called Salcombe Stone and has been used in the construction of Exeter Cathedral and several other local churches.

Triassic cliffs near Littlecombe Shoot. Fallen rocks on the beach contain fossil ripples which formed in temporary lakes within the desert.

Rocks in the wrong place?

The picturesque fishing village of Beer on the East Devon coast nestles in a natural bay surrounded by high cliffs of white Chalk. These rocks formed in shallow sub-tropical seas that covered East Devon and Dorset in the Cretaceous Period, over 70 million years ago. Most of the Chalk has since been eroded, but at Beer a quirk of geology has preserved it. This is because the Chalk rocks are folded and faulted downwards, level with the older rocks, and thus were protected from the erosion that was to come later. At Seaton, red Triassic rocks return and can be seen east of Seaton Hole.

BEER AND SEATON

Beer Quarry Caves

Just behind the village of Beer there is a layer of Chalk known as Beer Stone, composed of densely packed, minute shell fragments. This is a high quality masonry stone used in important buildings. Quarried from underground since Roman times, the workings have created Beer Quarry Caves which cover an area equivalent to over 50 football pitches. Guided tours are available.

Flint

The Chalk at Beer contains distinctive bands of flint. Although best known as a material for prehistoric tools, flint's durability has meant that it has been used as a local building stone in Beer and surrounding villages.

Hooken Landslide

Historical and recent views of the Hooken landslide near Beer, East Devon. The landslide occurred in 1789-90 and appears to have originated below sea-level. The drawing was made by Daniel Dunster in 1840 and the erosion between then and the present day can be seen by comparing the two images.

The Undercliff

The Axmouth to Lyme Regis Undercliffs National Nature Reserve is one of the most important wilderness areas in Britain. The entire reserve is formed from landslides, and is particularly famous for the occurrence of an enormous landslide at Bindon on Christmas Eve 1839. These landslides still occur today, creating an internationally important mix of habitats from dense scrub and woodland to open ground, with many special plants and animals. English Nature manage the reserve and visitors are required to keep to the South West Coast Path that runs through it. The journey on foot between Lyme Regis and Axmouth is an awe-inspiring and strenuous walk.

Goat Island and the chasm today.

The Bindon Landslide 1839

The Bindon Landslide became famous and attracted national publicity and thousands of visitors. People visited by paddle steamer and a piece of music, the Landslide Quadrille, was written for it. Many beautiful prints and engravings were made. Today they provide an invaluable record that shows how the environment has changed over time. Note in particular how woodland has colonised the area.

There are many historical landslides dating from at least the seventeenth century. The 1839 event was described by two eminent scientists of their day: William Conybeare, then the vicar of Axminster and William Buckland, professor of Geology at Oxford. Their work is possibly the earliest scientific description of a landslide and their explanation is still useful to current research.

The 1839 landslide is of a type known as a blockslide. A huge piece of land, known locally as Goat Island, moved towards the sea, leaving a deep chasm. The front edge of the landslide was uplifted out of the sea forming a small natural harbour. Although it proved to be a short-lived feature, questions were asked in Parliament about whether it could become a port for the Navy.

William Daniel Conybeare
(1787-1857)

William Buckland
(1784-1856)

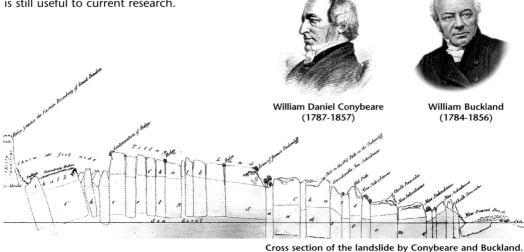

Cross section of the landslide by Conybeare and Buckland.

Mary Anning

Mary Anning (1799-1847) lived all her life in Lyme Regis and has been described as 'the greatest fossilist who ever lived'. She collected fossils at a time when scientific enquiry was leading to a change in the way people thought about the evolution of life and our planet - a story that would culminate with Charles Darwin's *On the Origin of Species*, published in 1859.

Mary collected fossils in the cliffs around Lyme and Charmouth as a child, working with her father Richard and her brother Joseph. Her father died when she was just 11 years of age, and Mary took on the family business, becoming the most skilled of collectors with an impressive knowledge of anatomy. Her record of fossil 'firsts' is remarkable, and resulted in many of the leading geologists of the day visiting the coast to learn from her work. Her achievements are all the more remarkable as she had no formal education.

Mary's extraordinary finds

Mary Anning, with her family, is responsible for a catalogue of exceptional fossil discoveries. They include the first ichthyosaur to come to scientific attention in 1814, the first complete plesiosaur in 1824, and the first British find of a flying reptile in 1828. She found countless other fossils of Jurassic marine animals. Her story is on display at the Lyme Regis Museum including her hammer (pictured). Many of her early, important finds are on display at the Natural History Museum in London.

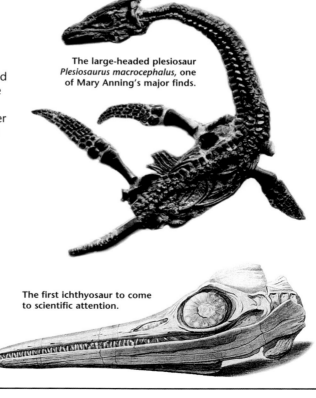

The large-headed plesiosaur *Plesiosaurus macrocephalus*, one of Mary Anning's major finds.

The first ichthyosaur to come to scientific attention.

Duria Antiquior - the first diorama

The image below is *Duria Antiquior* - a more ancient Dorsetshire. This is the first published scientific reconstruction of a past world. It was drawn by Henry de la Beche in 1830 and was inspired by the finds of Mary Anning. De la Beche was one of the major figures of early geology, founder of the British Geological Survey and a close friend of Mary Anning.

Sir Henry De la Beche (1796 -1855)

A *Scelidosaurus* reconstruction.

Recent discoveries

Mary Anning collected fossils over 200 years ago, and professional fossil collecting remains an important part of the modern life of the World Heritage Site. New and spectacular finds are still being made, mainly by local collectors. A recent important find is a near complete 3 metre skeleton of the dinosaur, *Scelidosaurus*, a species unique to Lyme Regis and Charmouth. Many separate pieces that make up the fossil were discovered over a period of two years.

The *Scelidosaurus* fossil found in 2000.

Fossils on the beach

Fossils are the remains of animals and plants that have been preserved in stone. They are the raw material for the science of palaeontology, and provide direct evidence of past life on Earth and the way in which it has changed over millions of years. The rocks that make up the cliffs at Charmouth are rich in fossils of animals that swam in the Jurassic seas. The coast erodes rapidly resulting in thousands of fossils being fed onto the beaches from the landslides in the surrounding cliffs, especially after winter storms. The remains that have been found here since the eighteenth century represent one of the richest slices of life in Jurassic times anywhere in the world.

Finding Fossils

Charmouth is the best and safest place to look for fossils in the World Heritage Site. Sharp eyes are the best tools for fossil hunting and it is recommended to look carefully amongst the rocks and pebbles on the beach when the tide is falling. Common finds are ammonites, belemnites, or possibly a fragment of ichthyosaur bone. The Charmouth Heritage Coast Centre is an essential part of any visit, and provides displays, information and advice on safe collecting.

➤ Ammonites have distinctive spiral shells.

◄ Belemnites were related to ammonites and had a straight body.

➤ Ichthyosaur vertebra is a more unusual find.

Spectacular preservation

One of the reasons the fossils found at Charmouth are exceptionally important is because the remains are often preserved in superb detail.

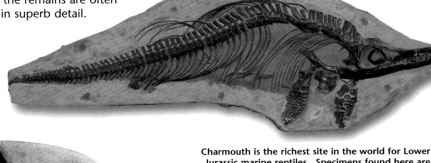

Charmouth is the richest site in the world for Lower Jurassic marine reptiles. Specimens found here are occasionally found preserved as complete skeletons.

The finds of small animals can be equally as spectacular as the large reptiles. This dragonfly was encased in fine mud at the bottom of the Jurassic sea, preserving every detail of its delicate wing structure.

FOSSIL COLLECTORS CODE OF CONDUCT & SAFETY

A fossil code of conduct is in operation on this stretch of coastline. Please keep away from the cliffs, and do not dig or hammer into them. **See Page 63.**

Tools of Time

Geologists are able to use fossils to help them identify rocks of similar age. Rocks which are hundreds of miles apart can be recognised as being of the same age due to the fossils they contain. Ammonites are especially good for the purpose as many evolved and changed rapidly (in geological terms), producing different species with distinctive shell forms. The Jurassic has been divided into a series of zones based on the appearance and disappearance of different ammonites. At Charmouth, rocks from 12 of these different ammonite zones can be found.

Dorset

Yorkshire

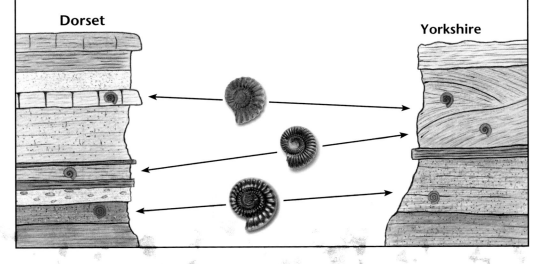

A National Treasure

Chesil is one of the finest barrier beaches in the world. It is made up of pebbles and shingle and has stood up to the full force of the Atlantic for thousands of years. It protects the Fleet, which is the largest tidal lagoon in Britain and a place of international importance for its birds and wildlife. Chesil and The Fleet are mostly owned by the Ilchester Estate.

The beach is over 17 miles (28 km) long and increases in height towards the east, reaching a maximum of over 15 metres near Portland. The pebbles also increase in size towards the east. At West Bay they are pea-sized while at Portland they are the size of baking potatoes. Local folklore claims that smugglers knew exactly where they had landed from the size of the pebbles on the beach. Pebbles move east along the beach driven by the action of the wind and waves. The grading of the pebbles may be because the larger pebbles move faster than smaller ones as the waves work on them.

The best places to appreciate the scale of the beach are from Abbotsbury and Portland. Visit the Chesil Beach Visitor Centre on the beach at Ferrybridge.

CHESIL AND THE FLEET

Yellow Horned Poppy.

Eelgrass.

Sea Pea.

The Fleet Lagoon

The Fleet Lagoon is a rich wildlife reserve which supports fresh, salt and brackish water species. Underwater there are extensive meadows of eelgrass, whilst strong currents at the mouth of the lagoon allow an exceptionally diverse mix of seaweed, sponges and anemones to flourish. A huge population of water birds rely on the lagoon. They include the oldest managed swan population in the world, which can be visited at the Abbotsbury Swannery.

Building the Beach

The origin of Chesil Beach remains the subject of debate. The traditional view is that the beach has been driven on shore by rising sea levels following the last Ice Age but the story might be more complex.

In the last interglacial period, about 125,000 years ago, sea levels were slightly higher than today and the landslides of West Dorset and East Devon were active. During the last Ice Age, sea levels dropped. The cliffs decayed into vast debris slopes that spilled across the exposed sea floor. With the end of the Ice Age about 10,000 years ago, rising sea levels reached these huge landslides, releasing a vast amount of chert and flint onto the shoreline. Longshore drift then carried the pebbles east, covering the beach that had been brought in by the rising sea and creating the massive structure we now see.

Today the beach is still moving on shore. After stormy weather, lumps of peat are washed ashore from the seaward side of the beach. They must be coming from sediments formed in a lagoon that lay further offshore when sea levels were lower over 4,000 years ago.

Portland Stone

The Isle of Portland is home to Portland Stone, probably the most famous building stone in the world. Many of London's finest buildings have been, and continue to be, built using this fine white limestone. The earliest known use was by the Romans. Christopher Wren famously chose the stone for the rebuilding of St. Paul's Cathedral after the Great Fire of London in 1666.

The stone was first worked from the landslides on the east coast. Quarrying followed at Portland Bill and at the northern end of the Island. The quarrymen worked the stone along huge natural fractures known as gullies which criss-cross the Island. They deposited the waste stone behind them, creating a unique landscape of drystone walls, tracks and quarry faces.

The story of the quarries is a unique and fascinating insight into the past and present stone industry. It is worth devoting time to explore the geology, archaeology, art and wildlife of the Island as well as visiting Portland Bill Visitor Centre and the Portland Museum.

Quarrying continues across the Island today. The approach is similar to the old days, working between the 'gullies', but modern machinery enables faster working. Two quarry viewing areas provide safe places to look at quarrying operations.

Portland sea lavender.

Pyramidal orchid.

Stonecrop.

Wildlife

The thin limestone soils support a rich flora and fauna, particularly orchids and butterflies. These are best seen in the late spring and early summer.

Sculpture in Tout Quarry.

Tout Quarry

The older quarries such as Tout and Kingbarrow contain an intimate mix of geology, stone heritage and wildlife which can be explored through a maze of footpaths. A wide range of sculptures have been carved in Tout Quarry which is open to the public.

The Isle of Portland

Folds and Faults

The World Heritage Site to the east of Weymouth provides interesting walking and beaches with unusual features. The coast is made up of a complex sequence of rocks, which have been jumbled up by geological folds and faults. The cliffs in this part of the World Heritage Site are formed from Upper Jurassic clays, limestones and sandstones.

The coast around Osmington is famous amongst geologists because of a natural seep of oil rising from the seabed. The rocks once formed an oil reservoir that has been breached by erosion. On a calm day, oil can still be seen seeping onto the surface of the sea near Bran Point, between Osmington Mills and Ringstead.

Diplocraterion is perhaps the most striking of all the trace fossils found here and forms large (30 cm) U shaped burrows with fine reworked sediment between the arms of the burrow.

Trace fossils

The coast around Osmington Mills is one of the best places to see trace fossils. These are the fossilised burrows and markings made by ancient marine animals. Several different trace fossils can be found on the beach and they provide evidence that the rocks formed in a shallow sea.

White Nothe - owned by the National Trust.

The massive cliff at White Nothe, east of Ringstead, is dominated by Cretaceous Chalk and sandstone, lying on top of Jurassic clays. A large, ancient landslide marches down the cliff face like a giant's staircase. A smaller slip in 1826 created the phenomenon known as 'Burning Cliff', when a chemical reaction caused the organic-rich clays to catch fire.

The rocks in this area are complexly folded and faulted. The steeply dipping strata form rock 'ribs' where eroded by the sea.

Osmington Mills.

Lulworth Cove

The beauty of the Purbeck Coast results from the way the power of the sea has acted on rocks of different resistance. At Lulworth Cove, limestone forms a massive bastion against the sea. A perfect horseshoe bay has developed where a stream breached the limestone, allowing the sea to enter the valley and hollow out the softer clays lying behind the limestone barrier. The Chalk forms a resistant cliff at the back of the bay. The Cove is one of the most famous features within the World Heritage Site, and is visited by thousands of schoolchildren every year. A visitor centre and exhibition is provided by the Lulworth Estate at the Cove.

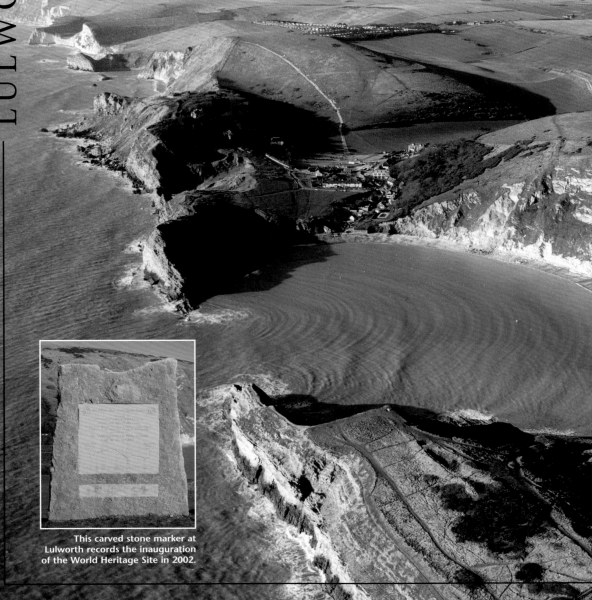

This carved stone marker at Lulworth records the inauguration of the World Heritage Site in 2002.

The Lulworth Crumple

Another bay is forming beside Lulworth Cove at Stair Hole. Here the breach has been made by collapsing caves and arches. This has revealed the famous 'Lulworth Crumple', a complex fold formed by major earth movements that occurred in the same period that the Alps were formed. A viewing platform has been provided to view the Crumple in safety.

How Lulworth Cove was formed

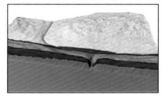

Stage 1
A stream breaches the bastion of resistant Portland Limestone.

Stage 2
The sea begins to erode the less resistant Wealden Beds behind the limestone.

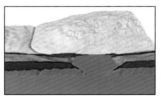

Stage 3
The bay widens as the sea erodes the Wealden rocks further on either side of the bay.

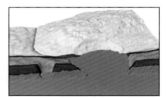

Stage 4
The sea reaches more resistant Chalk and forms the back wall of the bay with a steep landslipped cliff. The next bay begins to open at Stair Hole.

Durdle Door

Half a mile west of Lulworth Cove is Durdle Door - a perfect coastal arch. The rocks here have been tilted so they are almost vertical, and the limestone barrier has been almost destroyed. The arch shows how nature creates landforms that are self-supporting.

Reconstruction of the Fossil Forest. It grew at a time before the evolution of flowering plants, when conifers dominated world vegetation.

Jurassic 'Jungle'

Towards the end of the Jurassic period, about 144 million years ago, sea levels dropped and a series of islands emerged in Purbeck, surrounded by saline lagoons and channels. For a short period of geological time, soils formed and a tropical forest of giant cypress, monkey-puzzle trees, luxuriant cycads and ferns flourished. The forest was then flooded under a shallow, saline lagoon and thick mats of algae grew across the forest floor and around the base of the trees and fallen logs. Sediments stuck to the algae and built up over time to form large doughnut-shaped 'burrs' around the trees and wood. It is preserved today as the Fossil Forest, the most complete fossil record of a Jurassic forest in the world.

The Fossil Forest

The Fossil Forest is best seen to the east of Lulworth Cove, where it is displayed on a wide ledge in the cliff. The site lies within the Army Ranges and is subject to restricted opening times. The forest can also be seen on Portland and in quarries near Weymouth.

Fossil wood is no longer present at the Lulworth site, but is often uncovered during quarrying on Portland. When cut thinly and seen under the microscope, every detail of the wood structure can be seen. The irregularly spaced growth rings suggest trees grew in a climate where periods of drought alternated with wetter seasons.

Flowers Barrow

At Flowers Barrow the structure of Purbeck is dramatically displayed, with a ridge through the area formed by geological folding. Flowers Barrow is an Iron Age hill-fort, built 2,500 years ago. The effect of coastal erosion in the passing centuries is dramatically shown where a large part of the fort has been lost to the sea.

THE LULWORTH RANGES

Range Walks

The coast between Lulworth and Kimmeridge lies within a military firing range and access to the area is restricted. The range walks are open through most weekends of the year and during the main school holiday periods.

An International Name

The rocks at Kimmeridge Bay were once the floor of a deep, tropical sea rich in pre-historic life. They formed in the Jurassic period, 155 million years ago.

The cliffs and foreshore contain a very thick sequence of Kimmeridge Clay. The rock layers are like the pages in a book and the fossils they contain tell a story on each page. Each rock layer provides a window allowing us to look back through geological time. The sequence of rocks here provides such an excellent record of this part of the Jurassic that geologists have adopted Kimmeridgian as the term for rocks of this age all around the world.

Important fossils have been found in the Kimmeridge Clay, but they need an expert eye and time-consuming preparation. Hammering is strictly forbidden here and you may only collect loose fossils from the beach.

Kimmeridgien - a wine grown on Kimmeridgian age rocks in France.

Rocky ledges

Harder bands of limestone within the Kimmeridge Clay create a series of rocky ledges that run out to sea. As a result, the Bay boasts some of the most accessible marine wildlife in the UK. The stone ledges make it easy to view life on the shore and in the shallow waters, and there is safe snorkelling for the more adventurous. Kimmeridge Bay is part of the Purbeck Marine Wildlife Reserve, managed by the Dorset Wildlife Trust. The Trust runs the Fine Foundation Marine Centre in the bay, providing an exhibition, aquarium and a programme of events.

Oil in the rocks

The 'nodding donkey' on the cliff top has been producing oil since 1959. The oil formed in rocks that were laid down on a stagnant sea floor. The rocks were buried and organic matter within them was 'cooked' to form oil and gas. More oil lies in the northern part of Purbeck, and under Poole Harbour. This is the Wytch Farm Oilfield - the largest onshore oil field in the UK. It is difficult to see the carefully landscaped oil wells.

The geology of an oil field

Oil fields form where the structure of the rocks creates a trap for oil generated in the rocks below. At Kimmeridge the oil is held in the layer of rock called the Cornbrash which can also be found along the shore of the Fleet.

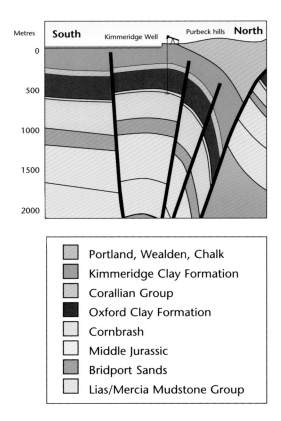

Portland, Wealden, Chalk
Kimmeridge Clay Formation
Corallian Group
Oxford Clay Formation
Cornbrash
Middle Jurassic
Bridport Sands
Lias/Mercia Mudstone Group

Kimmeridge Bay looking east towards Clavell's Tower.

Durlston Head

Durlston Head, topped by the splendid Victorian Durlston Castle (refurbished and reopened as an impressive Visitor Centre in 2011), offers exquisite views of the English Channel, Durlston Bay and the Isle of Wight. Parkland and wild coastal scenery is accessible to the public. Massive limestone cliffs run eastwards from St Aldhelm's Head. A geological fault has brought the Purbeck Limestones down to sea level, and the sea has created the landslipped coast of Durlston Bay in the softer rocks.

Wildlife on the coast

Durlston's downlands and meadows teem with wildflowers, birds and butterflies, whilst the south-facing limestone cliffs host an important seabird colony and nesting peregrine falcons. Regular sightings of bottlenose dolphins have been made. The Durlston Visitor Centre is open all year round. It provides information on daily wildlife sightings. In season there is live video coverage of the seabird colony and sounds are relayed from a hydrophone on the seabed in Durlston Bay.

George Burt

Managed today as a Country Park and National Nature Reserve by Dorset County Council, Durlston Park was the creation of George Burt of Swanage. Burt was part of the family that started the construction company, Mowlem. In 1862 he bought 80 acres of land in order to develop high-class residences, set in public landscapes and rejoicing in the spectacular environment. Burt failed to attract buyers for his planned residences, but many of the public works remain, including his great 'folly', Durlston Castle. Carved quotations around the Park set out Burt's vision of 'New Elysia' - a landscape shaped by a deep appreciation of nature. An example is:

" *An iron coast and angry waves*
  You seem to hear them rise and fall
  And roar rock thwarted in their billowing caves
  Beneath the windy wall."

The Great Globe

The Great Globe is the largest sculpture created by George Burt. Three metres in diameter and weighing some 40 tonnes, it is made from local Portland Limestone. The Great Globe shows the world in 1887. It is surrounded by stone plaques inscribed with astronomical data and quotations from poets and the scriptures.

A VISION OF NATURE

Ballard Down

The World Heritage Site ends just beyond the great Chalk headland of Ballard Down, and the sea stacks known as 'Old Harry Rocks'. The Chalk downland here is owned by the National Trust and managed for public access and wildlife. To the east, the Needles on the Isle of Wight are usually visible. These too are made of Chalk and only a few thousand years ago were connected to Ballard Down.

Viewed from the sea, the Chalk cliffs are even more dramatic and an unusual curved fault separates the vertical strata in Swanage Bay from the horizontal strata to the north.

Downland Wildlife

Ballard Down is a superb downland habitat. The wild Chalk flora is complemented by many species of butterfly, including Chalkhill Blue and Adonis Blue.

Stacks

At Old Harry Rocks, the dramatic effects of erosion by waves can be clearly seen. Waves attack the weak joints in the rock to form arches and caves. Eventually these collapse leaving isolated stacks like 'Old Harry'.

Formation of Stacks

Stage 1
An arch forms in the Chalk as the sea works into weaknesses in the rock.

Stage 2
The arch gradually enlarges as more and more Chalk is eaten away.

Stage 3
The arch eventually collapses into the sea, leaving the seaward pillar as an isolated stack.

Old Harry Rocks - Boat trips from Bournemouth Pier, Poole Quay and Swanage visit this part of the coast.

*'Look round and read
great nature's open book'*

Carved quotation at Durlston

VISITING THE JURASSIC COAST

Towns and villages provide access and facilities along the coast. The Site is accessible from the South West Coast Path and the sea. Please follow the safety and fossil codes which are in operation.

Visiting the Jurassic Coast

The Jurassic Coast is well served by its 'Gateway Towns' and villages which provide a good range of accommodation, museums and visitor centres throughout the area. Exeter, Bournemouth, Poole and Christchurch also provide a range of visitor facilities. There are mainline rail links to the area from London and Bristol. Exeter and Bournemouth airports are less than half an hour's journey from the coast.

Exploring the World Heritage Site is best done on foot or by sea. The entire Site is accessible via the South West Coast Path National Trail, which is easy to follow by looking for the acorn symbol. 🔱 A network of footpaths link to the coast path and make circular walks possible. Guided walks and events take place throughout the year and details can be found in tourist information centres and by logging onto www.jurassiccoast.org. All visitor centres and many museums offer regular walks, talks and other events.

There are numerous boat trip operators offering Jurassic Coast tours along the coast and this really is one of the best ways of seeing the Site. Tourist Information Centres have more details and boat trips are also usually advertised around local harbours and quaysides.

Public transport is available between many of the towns and villages which act as gateways to the Site. Please call 😊 Traveline on 0871 200 22 33 or visit www.traveline.info for specific public transport information.

SAFETY
On the beach and coast path
- Stay away from the base of the cliffs and the cliff top and ensure that children and dogs are kept under control.
- Do not climb the cliffs. Rockfalls can happen at any time.
- Beware of mudslides, especially during or after wet weather.
- Always aim to be on the beaches on a falling tide and beware of the incoming tide, especially around headlands. Be sure to check the tide tables.
- Beware of large waves in rough weather, especially on steeply shelving beaches.
- Observe all permanent and temporary warning signs; they advise on hazards and dangers. Check routes beforehand by visiting www.southwestcoastpath.com
- Be very careful on rocky foreshores which often have slippery boulders.
- Stay within your fitness level – some stretches of coast can be strenuous and/or remote.
- Make sure you have the right equipment for the conditions, such as good boots, waterproof clothing and sun screen if appropriate.
- Follow The Countryside Code.

Emergencies
In an emergency dial 999 or 112 and ask for the Coastguard, but be aware that mobile phone coverage in some areas is very limited.

FOSSILS
Collecting fossils
- The best, and safest place to look for fossils is on the beach, away from the base of the cliffs, where the sea has washed away soft clay and mud.
- Do not collect from or hammer into the cliffs, fossil features or rocky ledges.
- Keep collecting to a minimum. Avoid removing in situ fossils, rocks or minerals.
- The collection of specimens should be restricted to those places where there are plenty of fossils.
- Only collect what you need... leave something for others.
- Never collect from walls or buildings. Take care not to undermine fences, bridges or other structures.
- Be considerate and don't leave a site in an unsightly or dangerous condition.
- Do not use a hammer on flint or chert, which shatter into sharp fragments.
- Some landowners do not wish people to collect – please observe notices.

The West Dorset Fossil Collecting Code of Conduct
- This applies between Lyme Regis and Burton Bradstock.
- Collectors are asked NOT to dig in the cliffs without permission.
- Important fossil finds should be registered at the Charmouth Heritage Coast Centre.
- The full code is available from Charmouth Heritage Coast Centre or by logging onto www.charmouth.org

HAVE YOU MADE AN IMPORTANT FIND?
Tell us about it by contacting the nearest visitor centre or the World Heritage Team on

01305 224132
or visit

www.dorset.fossilcode.org

SAFETY & THE FOSSIL CODE

Visitor Centres and Museums (Some Centres open on a seasonal basis)

Fairlynch Museum, Budleigh Salterton	EX9 6NP	01395 442666
The Arches Jurassic Coast Interpretation Centre (on the seafront at Sidmouth)	–	–
Sidmouth Museum	EX10 8LY	01395 516139
Honiton Museum	EX14 1PG	01404 44966
Fine Foundation Centre (on the seafront at Beer)	–	–
Lyme Regis Philpot Museum	DT7 3QA	01297 443370
Jubilee Pavilion (on the seafront at Lyme Regis)		
Charmouth Heritage Coast Centre and Fine Foundation Education Centre	DT6 6LL	01297 560772
Bridport Museum	DT6 3NR	01308 458703
Fine Foundation Chesil Beach Centre	DT4 9XE	01305 206191
Portland Museum	DT5 1HS	01305 821804
Portland Bill Visitor Centre	DT5 2JT	01305 820495
Dorset County Museum, Dorchester	DT1 1XA	01305 262735
Lulworth Cove Heritage Centre	BH20 5RQ	01929 400587
Kimmeridge Marine Centre	BH20 5PF	01929 481044
Durlston Castle	BH19 2JL	01929 424443
Swanage Museum and Heritage Centre	BH19 2LJ	01929 421427
Studland Beach Visitor Centre	BH19 3AX	01929 450500
Wareham Town Museum	BH20 4NS	01929 553448

Tourist Information Centres (Some Centres open on a seasonal basis)

Exeter	EX1 1GF	01392 665700
Budleigh Salterton	EX9 6NG	01395 445275
Ottery St Mary	EX11 1BZ	01404 813964
Sidmouth	EX10 8XR	01395 516441
Honiton	EX14 1LT	01404 43716
Axminster	EX13 5AQ	01297 34386
Seaton	EX12 2TB	01297 21660
Lyme Regis	DT7 3BS	01297 442138
Bridport	DT6 3LF	01308 424901
Dorchester	DT1 1BE	01305 267992
Swanage	BH19 1LB	01929 422885
Wareham - Discover Purbeck	BH20 4LR	01929 552740
Poole	BH15 1HJ	0845 2345560
Bournemouth	BH1 2BU	0845 0511700
Christchurch	BH23 1AS	01202 471780

Other Useful Contacts

National Trust	West Dorset	01297 489481
	Devon	01392 881691
	Wiltshire & Dorset	01747 873250
	Purbeck	01929 450002
South West Coast Path Association		01752 896237
Natural England (Information on National Nature Reserves)		0300 06 06 000
Lulworth Army Range Office (Information on opening of Range Walks)		01929 404819
Geological information		www.dorsetrigs.org.uk
		www.devon.gov.uk/geology
Public transport information ☺ www.traveline.info		0871 200 22 33

For additional information please visit

www.jurassiccoast.org

Download the FREE Jurassic Coast App. and take a virtual Walk Through Time

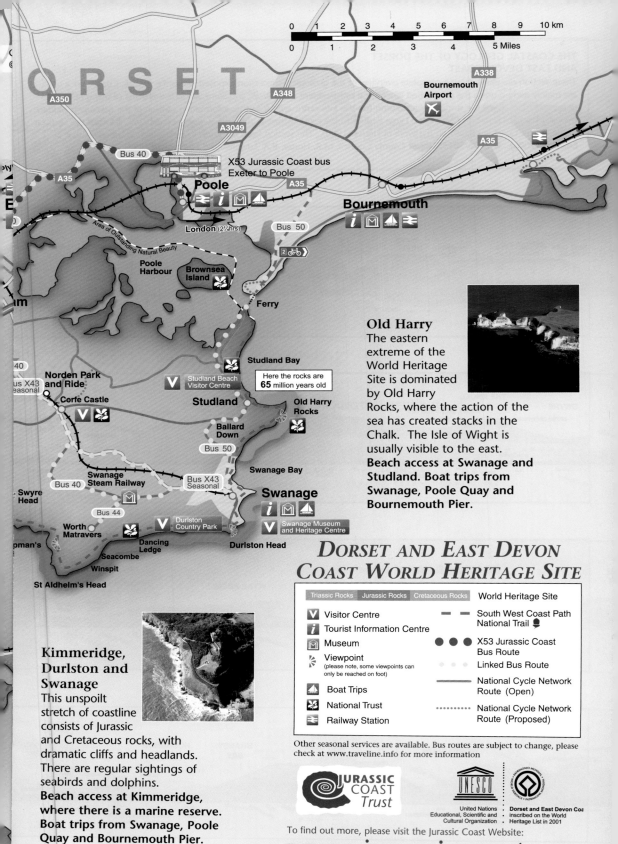

O R S E T

Poole

X53 Jurassic Coast bus
Exeter to Poole

Bus 40

Bournemouth

Bournemouth
Airport

A350 · A348 · A3049 · A35 · A338 · A35

London (2¼hrs)

Bus 50

Poole
Harbour

Brownsea
Island

Ferry

Studland Bay

Studland Beach
Visitor Centre

Here the rocks are
65 million years old

Studland

Old Harry
Rocks

Ballard
Down

Bus 50

Norden Park
and Ride

Corfe Castle

Bus X43
Seasonal

Swanage Bay

Swanage
Steam Railway

Bus X43
Seasonal

Swanage

Bus 40

Bus 44

Swanage Museum
and Heritage Centre

Swyre
Head

Worth
Matravers

Durlston
Country Park

Dancing
Ledge

Durlston Head

Seacombe

Winspit

St Aldhelm's Head

Chapman's

Old Harry

The eastern extreme of the World Heritage Site is dominated by Old Harry Rocks, where the action of the sea has created stacks in the Chalk. The Isle of Wight is usually visible to the east.
Beach access at Swanage and Studland. Boat trips from Swanage, Poole Quay and Bournemouth Pier.

Kimmeridge, Durlston and Swanage

This unspoilt stretch of coastline consists of Jurassic and Cretaceous rocks, with dramatic cliffs and headlands. There are regular sightings of seabirds and dolphins.
Beach access at Kimmeridge, where there is a marine reserve. Boat trips from Swanage, Poole Quay and Bournemouth Pier.

DORSET AND EAST DEVON COAST WORLD HERITAGE SITE

Triassic Rocks · Jurassic Rocks · Cretaceous Rocks · World Heritage Site

V Visitor Centre
i Tourist Information Centre
Museum
Viewpoint (please note, some viewpoints can only be reached on foot)
Boat Trips
National Trust
Railway Station

South West Coast Path National Trail
●●● X53 Jurassic Coast Bus Route
Linked Bus Route
National Cycle Network Route (Open)
National Cycle Network Route (Proposed)

Other seasonal services are available. Bus routes are subject to change, please check at www.traveline.info for more information

JURASSIC COAST Trust

UNESCO
United Nations Educational, Scientific and Cultural Organization

Dorset and East Devon Coast inscribed on the World Heritage List in 2001

To find out more, please visit the Jurassic Coast Website:

www.jurassiccoast.org

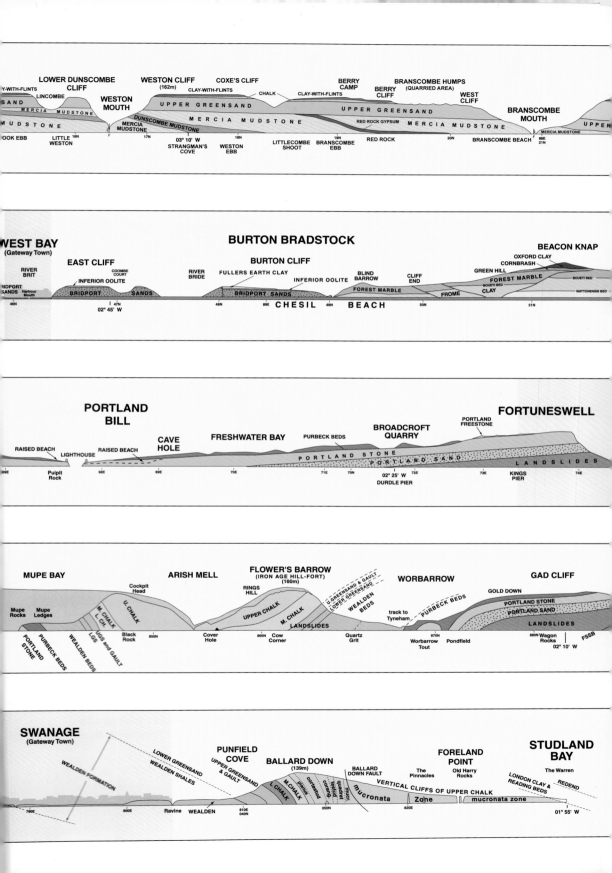